DINO-TREK

T0015725

BY SHALINI VALLEPUR

FOR A DIPLODOCUS

BookLife
PUBLISHING

©2022
BookLife Publishing Ltd.
King's Lynn
Norfolk PE30 4LS

A catalogue record for this book is available from the British Library.

ISBN: 978-1-80155-129-8

Written by:
Shalini Vallepur

Edited by:
Madeline Tyler

Designed by:
Danielle Webster-Jones

Photocredits:

Images are courtesy of Shutterstock.com.
With thanks to Getty Images, Thinkstock Photo and iStockphoto.

Front Cover - Luis Louro 2 - I Wei Huang. 4 - Luis Louro.
5 - paleontologist natural. 6 - GOLFX. 7 - Elnur. 8 – Herschel Hoffmeyer. 9 - Freer, Christos Georghiou, . 10 - Smithsonian Institution from United States [No restrictions], via Wikimedia Commons, Shor [Public domain], via Wikimedia Commons. 11 - Art by A. Atuchin. Published by D. Cary Woodruff, Thomas D. Carr, Glenn W. Storrs, Katja Waskow, John B. Scannella, Klara K. Nordén & John P. Wilson. [CC BY 4.0 (https://creativecommons.org/licenses/by/4.0)], via Wikimedia Commons. 12 - U.S. National Park Service, restoration/cleanup by Matt Holly [Public domain], via Wikimedia Commons. 13 -paulaphoto, Newtonian.
14 - Vasilyev Alexandr. 15 - Wlad74. 16 - Freer Marysha. 17 - N-sky, cjchiker. 18–19 - Sgoran cakmazovic, LegART. 20 - Et3e. 21 - Gelpi, Catmando. 22 - Heinrich Harder (1858-1935) [Public domain], via Wikimedia Commons.
23 - Luis Louro, Linda Bucklin.

CoNTeNTS

WELCOME TO THE DINO-TREK!

It is time to see some dinosaurs! You will become a palaeontologist and go on an adventure looking for dinosaur fossils.

A palaeontologist is a scientist who studies what life on Earth was like before we humans came around. They go on excavations where they dig up the ground looking for fossils.

WHAT ARE FOSSILS?

A fossil is made when an animal or plant is preserved in rock. The hard parts, such as bone or shell, are left behind. They leave a shape in the rock for us to study. Dinosaur fossils are millions of years old.

Palaeontologists study fossils from animals, plants and bacteria. They must be very careful not to break or damage fossils. They wear gloves to handle fossils and gently brush away dirt.

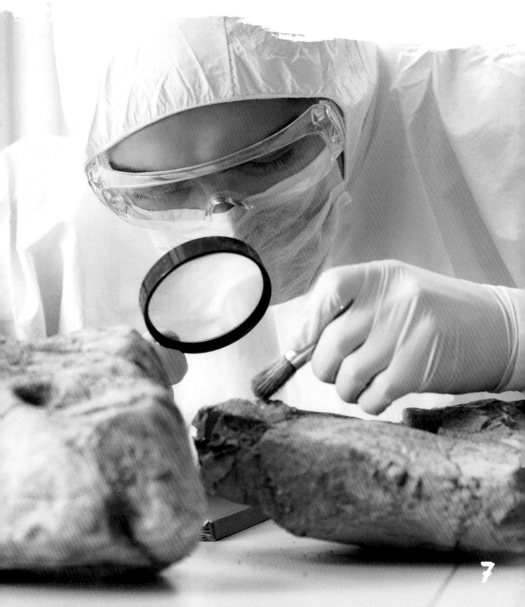

DIPLODOCUS

Diplodocus was a type of dinosaur called a sauropod. It had a huge neck and a long tail.

Diplodocus lived around 153 million years ago. From the end of its snout to the tip of its tail, Diplodocus could grow to around 30 metres long.

PALAEONTOLOGISTS OF THE PAST

Palaeontologists Earl Douglass and Samuel Williston first discovered Diplodocus fossils in 1877. It must have been amazing to find such a big fossil.

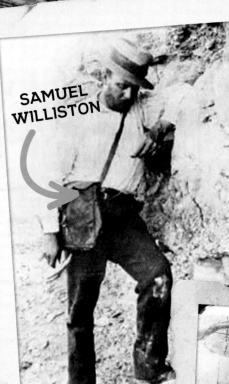

SAMUEL WILLISTON

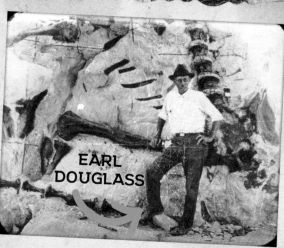

EARL DOUGLASS

Andrew the Diplodocus

In 2010, the fossil of a young Diplodocus was found. He was named Andrew. Although Andrew was young, he was already a massive six metres long!

LET'S DIG

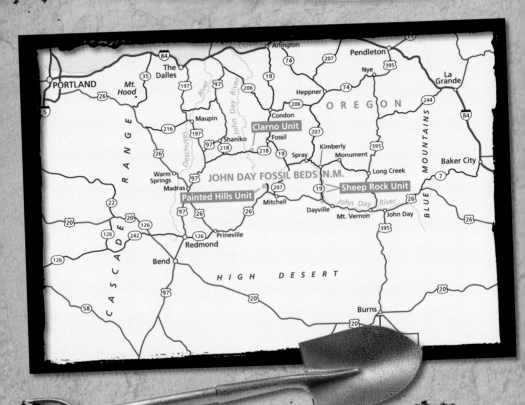

We have to find a good site to excavate. Palaeontologists cannot just dig wherever they want to. We can use fossil maps to show us where fossils have been found before.

We can think about Diplodocus's habitat, too. It is believed that Diplodocus lived in flat, grassy plains and areas of woodland where the US is today.

GREEDY EATERS

Is there something buried in the ground? It needs to be gently removed using a spade so we can clean it and get a closer look.

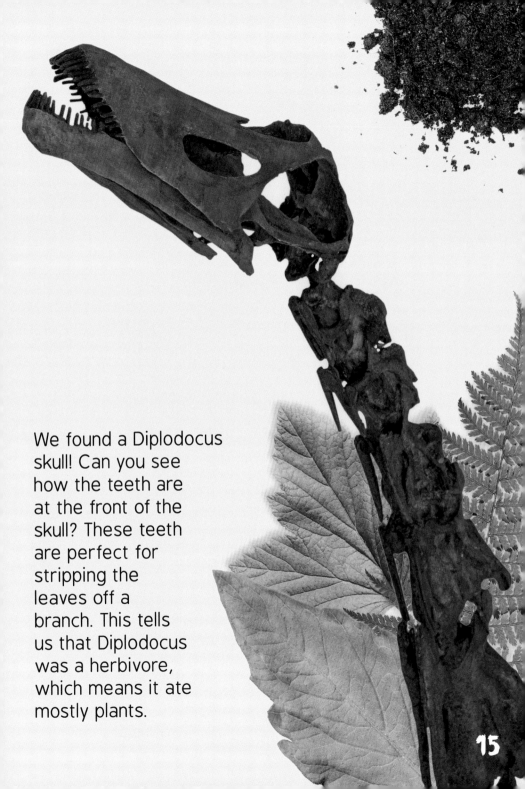

We found a Diplodocus skull! Can you see how the teeth are at the front of the skull? These teeth are perfect for stripping the leaves off a branch. This tells us that Diplodocus was a herbivore, which means it ate mostly plants.

Diplodocus was very big, so it had to eat a lot of plants. Palaeontologists think that Diplodocus removed leaves from plants and trees in one single swipe.

It is thought that Diplodocus swallowed stones to smash up plants in its stomach. Stones that are swallowed like this are called gastroliths.

CRACK THAT WHIP

If you look closely, you might notice that Diplodocus's tail is longer than its neck. But why was its tail so long?

Diplodocus's tail was made up of around 80 bones. It used its long tail to help it balance its neck and body to stand up straight. It could also whip its tail to make terrifyingly loud booming noises.

FOLLOW THE FOOTSTEPS

It might be hard to see, but this is a dinosaur trackway. These trackways are usually footprints that have been preserved over time. This one looks like it could have been made by Diplodocus.

We think that Diplodocus travelled around in groups called herds. Sauropod trackways have been found that show that adult sauropods and young sauropods stayed together.

THINK AGAIN

Sometimes palaeontologists get things wrong at first. Many people believed that Diplodocus crawled around like a lizard with its belly on the floor. Palaeontologists now know that this is not true.

There is still a lot to discover as a palaeontologist. New fossils are being excavated and studied all the time. Maybe you could be the next palaeontologist to discover a sauropod as delightful as Diplodocus.

QUESTIONS

1: What did Diplodocus eat?

2: How long ago was Diplodocus alive?
a) 153 years ago
b) 153 thousand years ago
c) 153 million years ago

3: How long was Andrew the Diplodocus?

4: What did Diplodocus do with its long tail?

5: What is your favourite dinosaur?

BookLife
freedom
Readers